BASS TABS
Bass Lines, Riffs and Tunes

by Laurence Harwood

Edited by Dan Wright

Guitar Command

www.GuitarCommand.com

Published by Timescale Music

ISBN: 978-0-9556566-7-5

Index

Introduction

The aim of this book is to provide beginner and intermediate bass guitarists with not only some great music to play but also with the tools they need to create their own bass lines.

Section 1

The first section of this book contains a selection of example songs. These have been written in a variety of musical styles, and give an idea of the kind of bass lines a bassist can play under a chord progression.

Section 2

The second section of this book contains a large number of bass riffs and patterns. These can be used to build up a library of bass ideas that you can use in a variety of musical situations.

Section 3

The third part of the book contains famous tunes arranged for bass guitar. Being a bass guitarist isn't all about playing root notes – there is plenty of opportunity to take the limelight now and again! Use these melodies to perfect your technique and also to play to family and friends.

Guitar chords are provided in sections 1 and 3.

As well as providing material that will hopefully be inspiring and technique-building, all of the songs, patterns and tunes in this book can also be used to improve your sight-reading.

Free Companion MP3s

A free companion MP3 album for this book can be downloaded from:

www.guitarcommand.com/bass-tabs-mp3s/

The album contains recordings of all of the pieces in this book, plus backing tracks for the song examples in section 1. It is not essential that you have the album, especially if you are working through the book with a tutor or have some knowledge of reading musical rhythms.

Guitar Command Bass Backing Tracks

Guitar Command also produce a range of bass backing track albums. Use these to invent your own bass lines and to improvise bass solos.

Hear samples at **www.GuitarCommand.com**

How To Read TAB

Tab is a system of writing out music for fretted instruments that has been in use for hundreds of years. Tab is short for 'tablature', but most musicians just use the shortened form of the word.

Tab is easier for beginners to read than traditional musical notation and can be learned very quickly. However, it does have limitations, and many bassists also learn to read standard notation. A brief guide to reading notated rhythms is also provided in this book.

How Tab Works

In tab parts, the horizontal lines represent the strings, and the numbers show the frets at which notes should be played. Tab for a standard four string bass guitar has four horizontal lines, one for each string.

In tab, a zero shows that the string should be played open, i.e. without any notes being held down.

Tab is usually provided on a separate line underneath standard notation.

The music below shows the open strings of a bass guitar in tab.

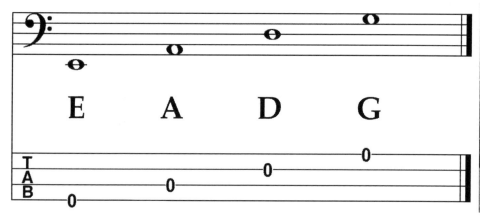
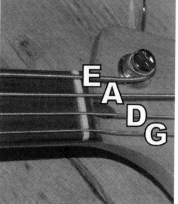

Notes In Tab

To play the G shown below, play the E string fretted at the 3rd fret.

To play the A shown below, play the G string fretted at the 2nd fret.

Try playing a G major scale by following the tab below.

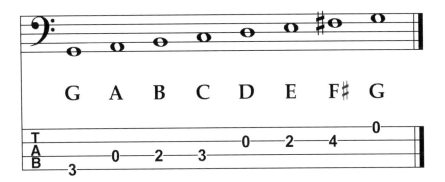

Bar Lines

Bar lines appear in tab as vertical lines, exactly as they do in standard notation. Bar lines break up the music into bars. The number of beats in a bar is shown in the time signature (see next section).

Rhythms In Tab

The main drawback with tab is that it does not show rhythms very accurately: it shows where the notes should be played, but not how long they are. For this reason tab is most effective when used alongside notation.

Because tab numbers are positioned directly below their notation counterparts, and notation is usually spaced (roughly) according to the rhythm of the music, tab does give some indication of the rhythm. If you already know the piece, or you have a good ear, then you can often get by. However, having even a basic knowledge of notation will be an immense help when reading tab.

There are many excellent books on reading music if you wish to go down this path. As an introduction, the basic elements of rhythmic notation are provided on the following pages.

Rhythmic Notation

The basic types of note are shown below, together with their durations.

Rests

In music, it is just as important to know when to stop playing as it is when to start. In music notation, symbols called 'rests' are used to tell a musician not to play anything, or to stop any notes that are already sounding. Common rest symbols and their durations are shown below, next to the notes with the same duration.

Notes	Value	Rests
	Sixteenth	
	Eighth	
	Quarter	
	Half	
	Whole	

Tied Notes

A curved line joining two notes of the same pitch means that they are 'tied'. Only the first note is played, and is held for the total duration of both of the tied notes. The illustration shows tied quarter notes. The first note would be played, and held for the total duration of both notes (i.e. for two quarter notes).

Groups of more than two notes can be tied, making even longer notes.

Dotted Notes And Rests

A dot immediately after a note or a rest increases its duration by half again. For example, a dotted quarter note has a duration of one and a half quarter notes.

Dotted Notes & Rest

Time Signatures

Time signatures show how the music is counted. They consist of two numbers, one on top of the other, written at the beginning of a piece of music. The most commonly used time signature in popular music is 4/4. This means that there are four quarter beats to a bar.

The upper number shows how many beats there are in each bar, the lower number shows the duration of each beat. Some commonly used time signatures are shown opposite.

3/4 time. Three quarter note beats in a bar. Counted 'One, Two, Three'.

 4/4 time. Four quarter note beats in a bar. Counted 'One, Two, Three, Four'.

 6/8 time. Six eighth notes, counted in two groups of three. This means that each bar has two main beats, counted: 'One-two-three, one-two-three'.

 12/8 time. Twelve eighth notes, counted in four groups of three. Each bar has four main beats, counted 'One-two-three, one-two-three, one-two-three, one-two-three'.

Bass Guitar Fret Notes Chart

Use this chart to learn the notes on the bass fretboard. After the twelfth fret, the notes repeat an octave higher.

Fret Number	Notes			
Open	E	A	D	G
1	F	A#/Bb	D#/Eb	G#/Ab
2	F#/Gb	B	E	A
3	G	C	F	A#/Bb
4	G#/Ab	C#/Db	F#/Gb	B
5	A	D	G	C
6	A#/Bb	D#/Eb	G#/Ab	C#/Db
7	B	E	A	D
8	C	F	A#/Bb	D#/Eb
9	C#/Db	F#/Gb	B	E
10	D	G	C	F
11	D#/Eb	G#/Ab	C#/Db	F#/Gb
12	E	A	D	G

Section 1: Songs

This section of the book contains a selection of example songs. They have been written to demonstrate typical bass lines in a number of rock and pop genres. Most have a basic, two-section structure, to illustrate how a bassist often has to play a different bass pattern for each part of a song, e.g. verse and chorus.

Many of these basslines are pattern-based - that is, they are made up of repeating riffs that follow the chord progression. Section 2 of this book contains a large number of bass riffs that you can use to create your own bass lines.

Song Structure

Most of the songs have two main parts. All repeats are optional: you can play the songs as written, play the songs twice before ending, or play straight through without repeating any of the sections.

You can hear recordings of these songs on the companion album. The album also contains backing tracks without the bass guitar part, allowing you to play each song as if you were the bassist in the band.

On the companion album, the songs are played twice through before ending.

Repeat Signs

Repeat:

go back to previous forward repeat sign or to beginning.

Forward Repeat:

repeat from here.

A repeat sign means that you should return to the previous forward repeat sign, and play the section again. If there is no forward repeat sign, then you should return to the beginning of the piece.

First And Second Endings

Repeated sections may have first and second endings. When this occurs, play the first ending the first time, and the second ending on the repeat.

Minor Song

Slow and steady

Tight Rhythm

Moderate

50's Style

Rhythm And Blues

Medium tempo

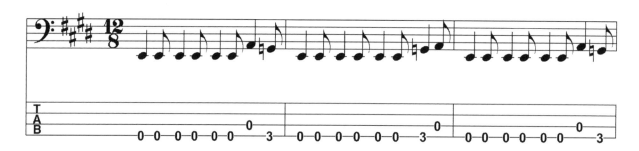

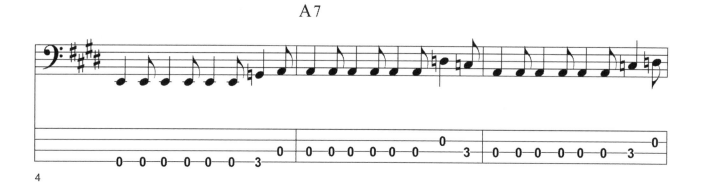

Walking Bass Blues

Moderate

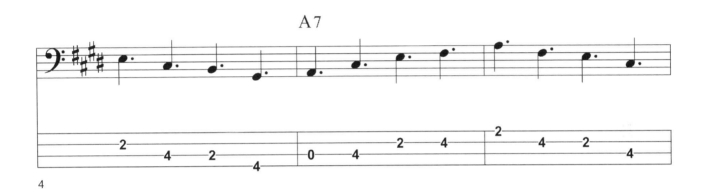

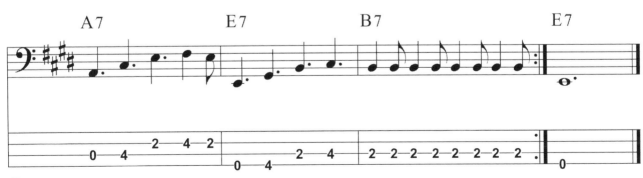

13

Slowdown

Country Waltz

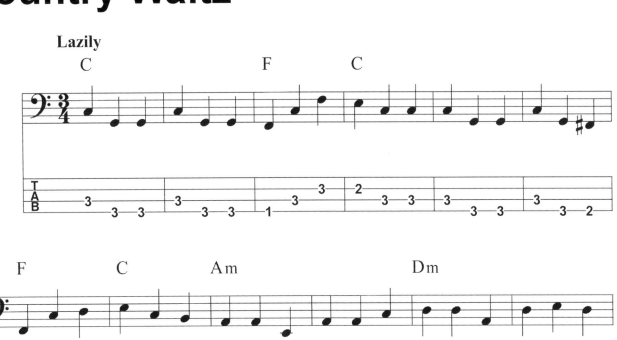

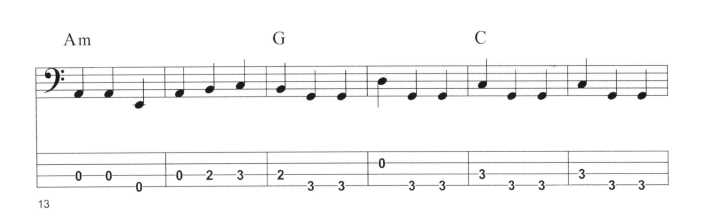

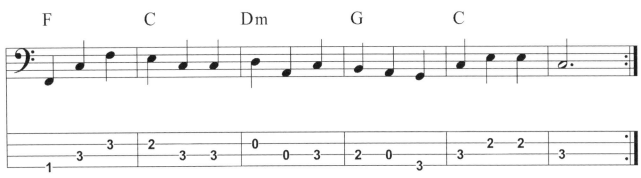

Indie Swing

Cool Indie

Driving Song

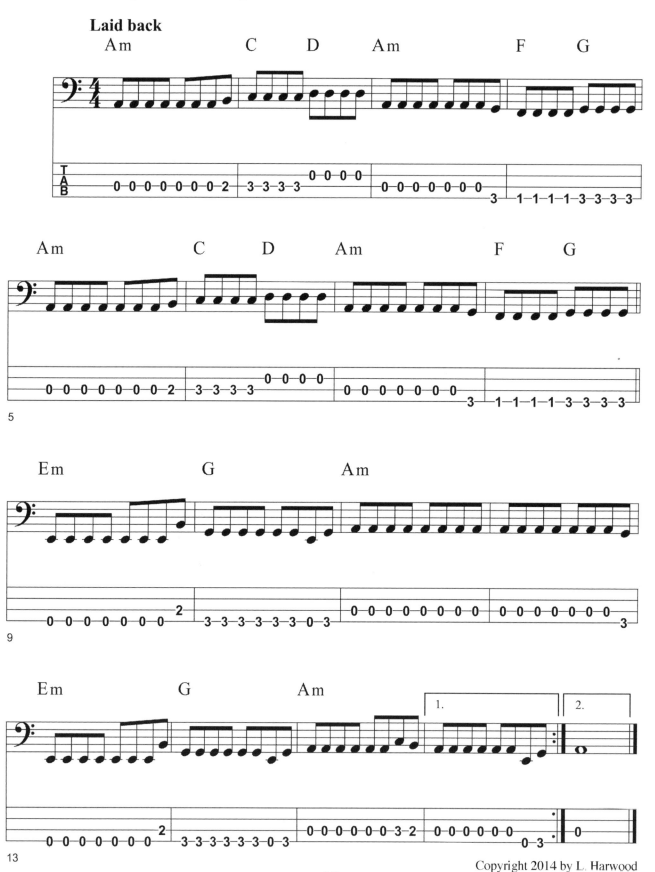

Metal Groove

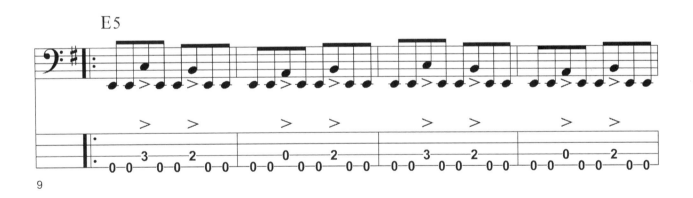

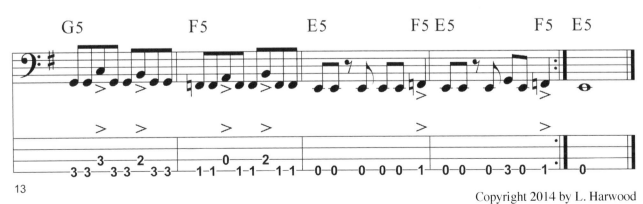

Melodic Rock

Moderately fast

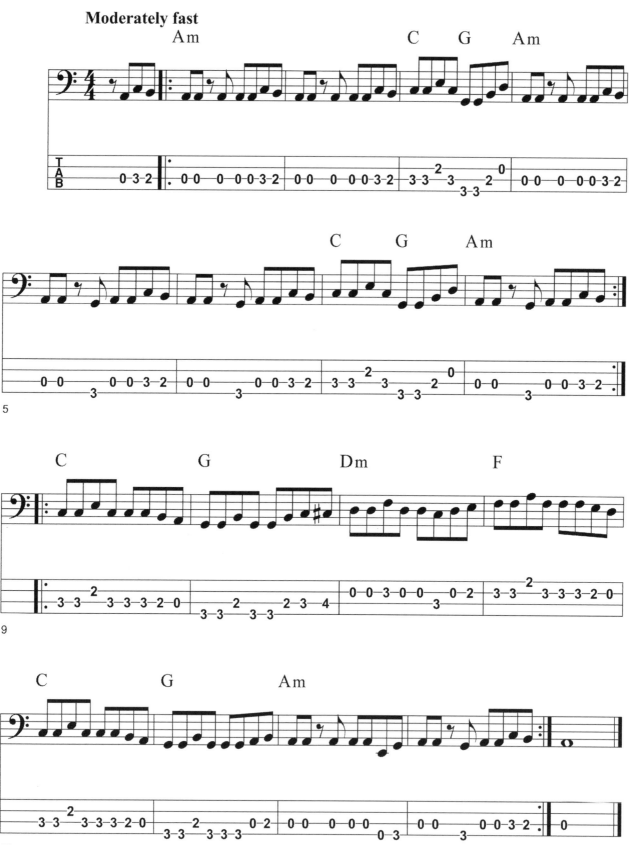

Surf Rock

Funk Bass

Slow groove

3

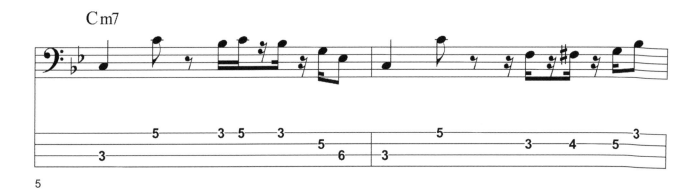

5

7

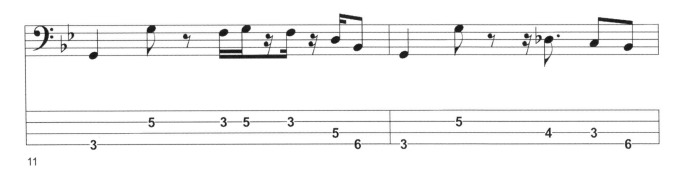

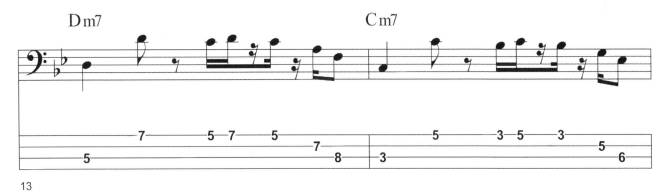

23

Secret Agent

Slow groove

4

7

10

Fast Metal

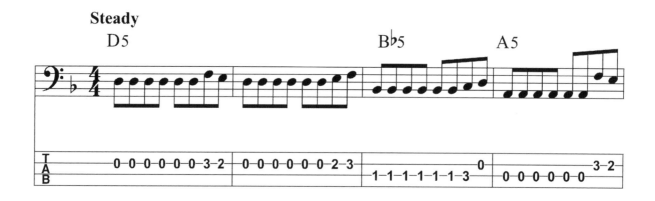

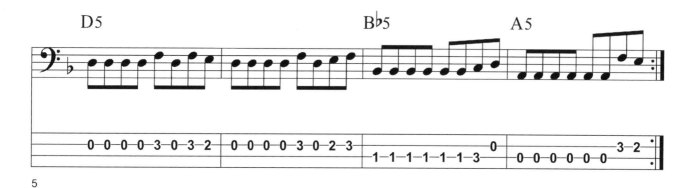

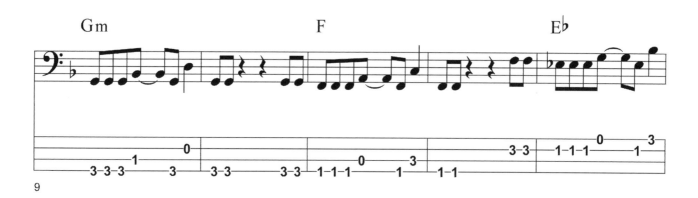

26

Chart Bass

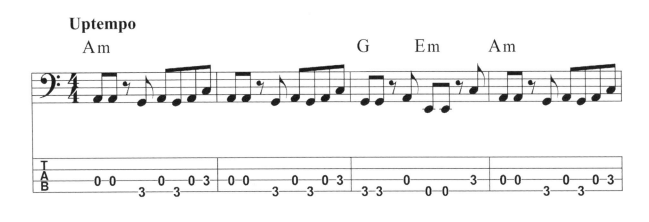

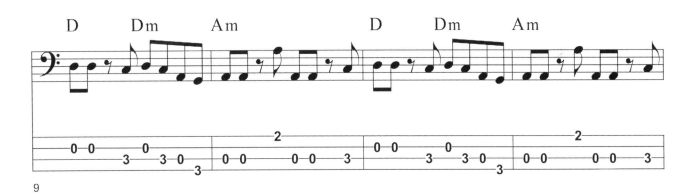

27

The Fighter

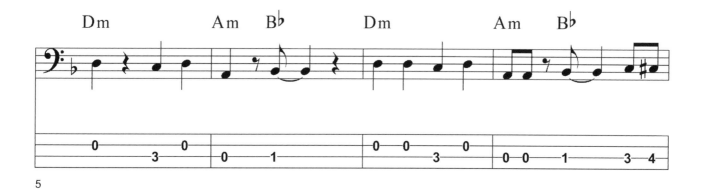

5

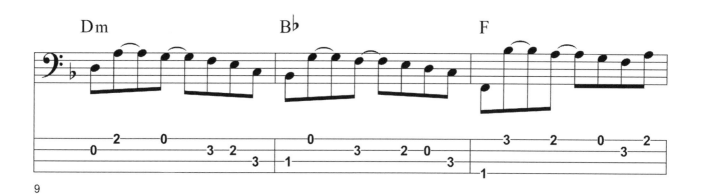

9

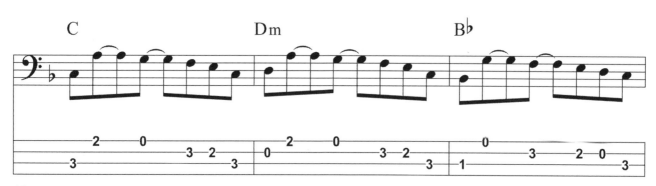

12

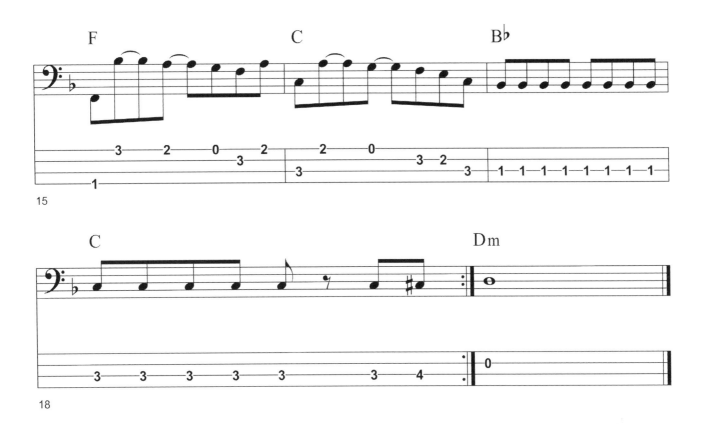

Folk Ballad

Sequenced Bass

Mid tempo

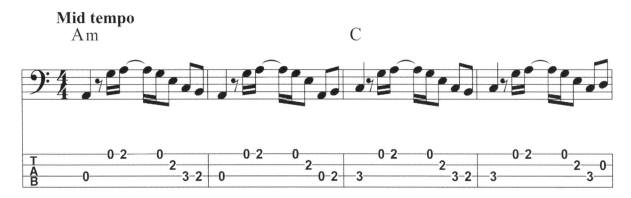

5

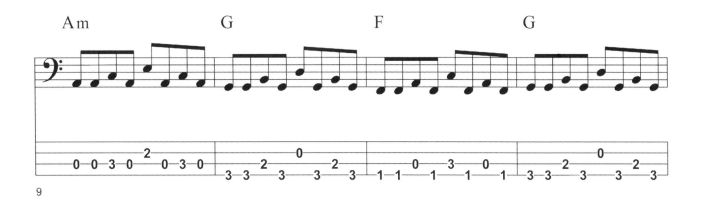

9

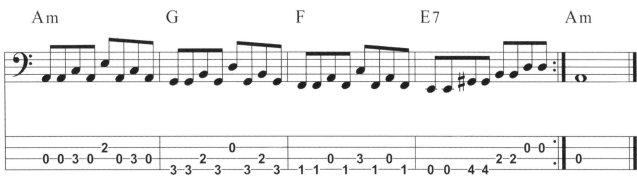

13

Bass Riffs

This section of the book contains a large number of bass riffs. You can play them unaltered, or use them as a starting point for creating your own grooves and bass lines. The patterns get gradually more complex throughout the section. Jam with them, alter them, transpose them or simply use them to improve your sight reading.

Each riff in this section can either be used separately, or as part of a longer bass line with multiple sections.

Most of the riffs are two bars long. If you like the pattern but only need a one-bar riff, simply split the pattern into two, and use either the first or second bar.

Many of the riffs are standard throughout a range of musical styles: you should be able to find a suitable one for the song you wish to play.

The following information is provided for each riff:

Root note (e.g. C); tonality (major or minor, sometimes both); style (e.g. rock); suggested tempo.

Note that the style and tempo are purely suggestions: you may find that a fast 'metal' pattern also works very well with a laid-back chart song.

Bass Line Construction - A Brief Guide

There are many kinds of bass line, and there are no hard and fast rules saying how they should be constructed.

Some songs have the same bass riff all of the way through, perhaps with small variations for verses, choruses, etc. Others will have different bass patterns for each of the various parts of the song.

Some bass lines follow the chords of the song, and move around with the chord progression. Others take the form of an unchanging groove, with the other instruments suggesting the chord changes.

Groove-Based Songs

Many groove-based songs are written in a jam situation. With the rhythm section (e.g. you and a drummer) creating an underlying groove, the other instruments (guitar, keyboards, etc.) play chords and melodies that fit over the top of the bass line. This is the 'bottom-up' approach. To create this kind of song, you could start with a bass pattern and get a groove going with a drummer. The other instruments in the band could play suitable chords, melodies or supply other rhythmic elements. You can add variations as you go in order to maintain interest or to underline changes in the song.

Transposing Bass Patterns To Create Lines And Songs

An alternative to the groove-based approach is a chord-based approach. You can do this by using one of the patterns in this book and moving it around the fretboard to suggest chord changes. For example, by playing a D major pattern in the original position, then moving it down two frets and playing it in C major, before returning to the original position.

The illustrations below show a bass riff in D, followed by the same riff played in C. Notice how the fingers play the same frets in relation to each other.

Bass patterns can be transposed not only by being moved up and down the fretboard, but also by being moved across to other strings. For example, by moving a pattern that originally started on the third string over to the fourth string. All of the other notes in the pattern should be moved relative to the first note. In this case, if the original pattern was in D, then the new pattern would be in A.

Sometimes moving patterns in this way will cause notes to 'fall off' of the fretboard. If this happens then the pattern will need to be altered, perhaps by playing the problem notes an octave lower or higher, or by substituting them with different notes. Remember, you should be using the patterns as a starting point for your own lines, and you should be using your ears to judge the effectiveness of your bass lines at all times.

Following Chord Progressions

To follow an existing chord progression, you can often transpose the bass riff to follow the root notes of the chords. For example, if the chord progression is: Gm, Cm, Dm, Gm, then you could try moving a minor key pattern up or down the fingerboard to follow the chords.

However, this does not always fit with the song, and most chord progressions use a mixture of major, minor and other chord types. This means that you will have to vary the bass pattern slightly to fit with individual chords. The exact harmonic process for doing this is beyond the scope of this book, but sometimes the bassist can simply alter any thirds contained in a riff to make it fit with the chord.

For example, if the bass riff contains a minor third and you want to play it with a major chord, then you can raise the minor third in the riff a half tone (one fret) to make it a major third.

If all this talk of minor and major thirds makes you break out in a cold sweat, then don't worry. Although reading up on musical harmony is always beneficial, you can simply do what many other musicians do and use your ears to alter and adapt bass patterns to create effective bass lines.

Try following the chord progressions from the songs in section 1 of this book using riffs from section 2.

Follow The Bass Drum

One technique for creating effective bass lines is to play patterns that emphasize the bass drum rhythm. Alternatively, have the drummer play rhythms that fit with the bass guitar part. Working with the drummer to produce complementary parts gives the rhythm section a tightness that will make the whole band sound better.

1.

A Minor
(or A Major)
Pop
Medium

2.

A Minor
Rock
Medium / Fast

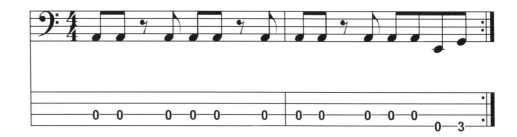

3.

A Minor
Pop
Medium / Slow

4.

G Minor
(or G Major)
Rock
Medium / Fast

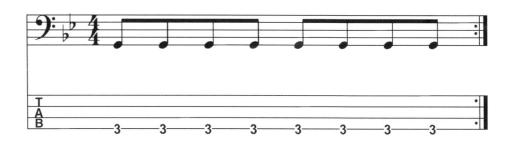

5.

G Minor
Rock
Medium

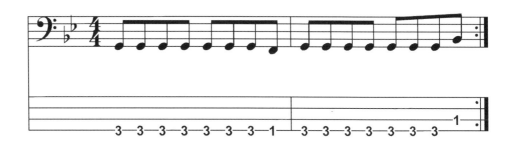

6.

G Minor

Rock

Medium / Slow

7.

C Minor
(or C Major)

Pop

Medium

8.

D Minor

Pop

Medium

9.

C Major

Pop

Slow

10.

F Major
(or F Minor)

Pop

Medium

11.
D Minor
Metal
Medium / Slow

12.
A Minor
Rock
Medium

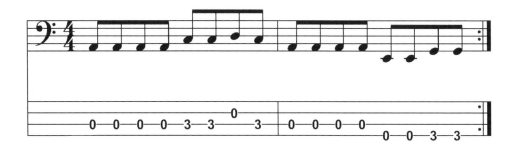

13.
A Minor / Major
Pop
Medium

14.
G Minor
(or G Major)
Rock
Medium / Fast

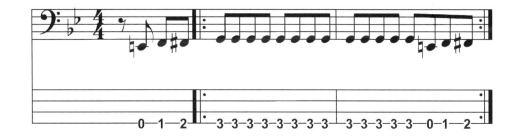

15.
G Minor
Metal
Medium / Fast

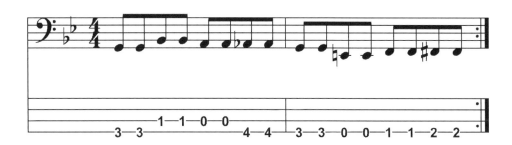

16.
C Minor
Rock
Medium

17.
C Minor
Pop
Medium / Fast

18.
C Minor
Rock
Medium

19.
G Major
Pop
Medium / Fast

20.
D Major
Rock
Medium / Fast

21.
F Major
Rock
Medium / Slow

22.
F Major
Rock
Medium

23.
C Minor
Rock
Medium

24.
A Major
Rock
Medium

25.
C Major
Pop
Medium / Slow

26.

A Minor
(or A Major)

Pop

Medium

27.

C Major

Pop

Medium / Slow

28.

A Major
(or A Minor)

Pop

Medium

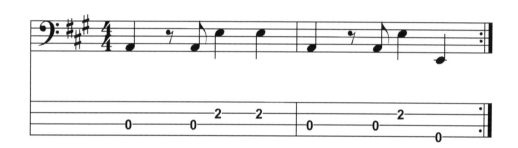

29.

A Minor

Rock

Medium / Fast

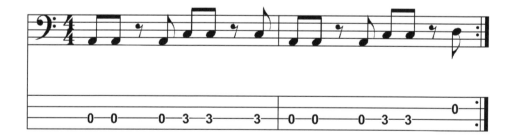

30.

A Major

Pop

Medium

31.
A Major
Pop
Medium

32.
G Major
(or G Minor)
Pop
Medium

33.
G Major
Pop
Medium

34.
F Major
Pop
Medium

35.
D Major
Pop
Medium

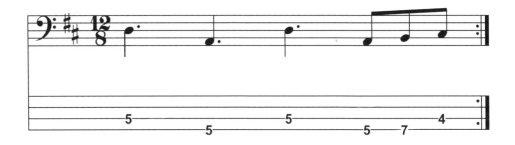

36.
A Major
Blues
Medium

37.
A Major
Blues
Medium / Slow

38.
Bb Major
Blues
Medium

39.
E Minor
Blues
Medium / Slow

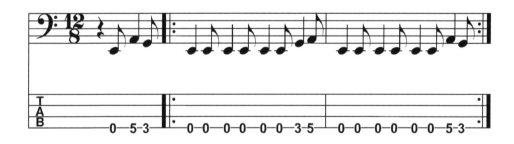

40.
A Minor
Blues
Medium

41.
G Minor
Blues
Medium

42.
C Minor
Rock
Medium

43.
A Minor
Funk
Medium / Fast

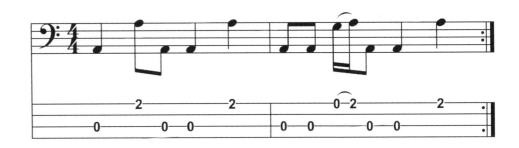

44.
A Minor
Pop
Medium / Fast

45.
A Minor
Metal
Medium

46.
A Minor
Metal
Medium / Fast

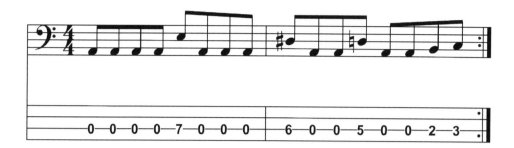

47.
A Minor
Rock
Medium / Slow

48.
G Minor
Pop
Medium / Fast

49.
G Minor
Metal
Medium / Fast

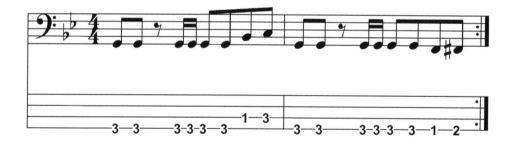

50.
C Minor
(or C Major)
Rock
Medium

51.
C Minor
Rock
Medium

52.
D Minor
Rock
Medium / Fast

53.
C Minor
Pop
Medium / Fast

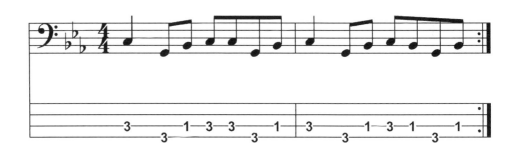

54.
C Minor
Metal
Medium

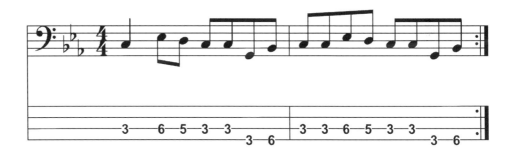

55.
F Minor
Funk
Medium

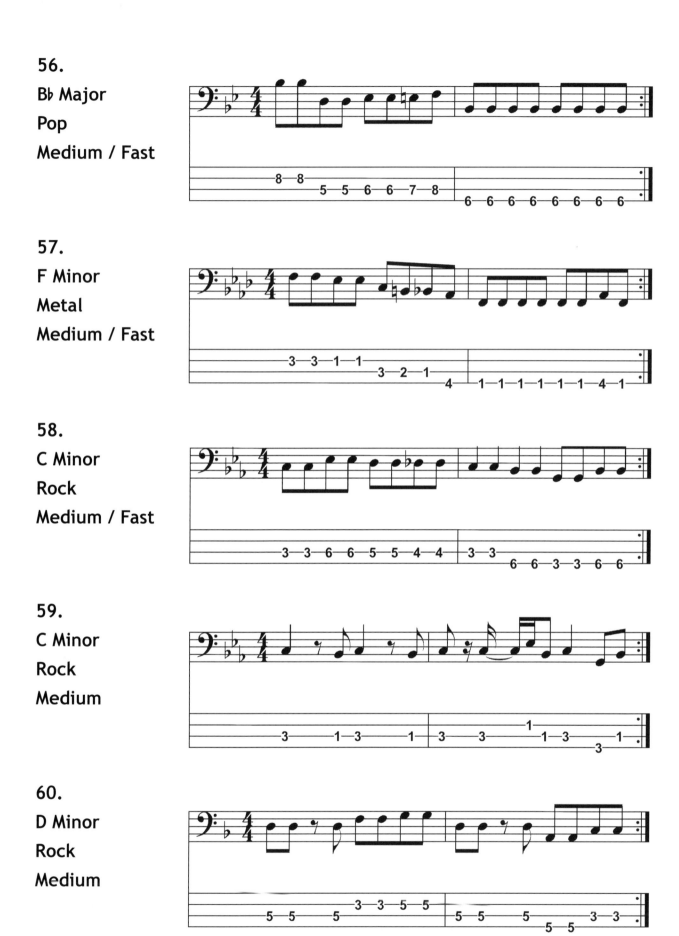

61.
C Minor
Rock
Medium / Fast

62.
A Major
Pop
Medium

63.
F Major
(or F Minor)
Rock
Medium / Slow

64.
D Major
Pop
Medium

65.
A Minor
(or A Major)
Metal
Medium / Fast

66.

A Major

Blues

Medium

67.

A Major

Blues

Medium

68.

B♭ Major

Blues

Medium / Fast

69.

G Major

Blues

Medium

70.

G Major

Blues

Medium

71.
A Major
Blues
Medium

72.
C Minor
Pop
Medium

73.
F Minor
Metal
Medium

74.
D Minor
Blues
Medium / Fast

75.
C Minor
Blues
Medium

76.
D Major
Pop
Medium / Fast

77.
D Minor
Pop
Medium

78.
C Major
Pop
Medium / Fast

79.
C Minor
Rock
Medium

80.
D Minor
Rock
Medium / Fast

81.
Bb Major
Pop

82.
A Minor
Rock
Medium

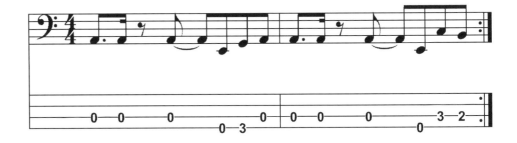

83.
G Minor
Metal
Medium / Fast

84.
G Minor
Funk
Medium

85.
C Minor
Rock
Medium

86.
C Minor
Funk
Medium / Slow

87.
G Major
Pop
Medium / Slow

88.
G Major
Pop
Medium

89.
F Major
Rock
Medium

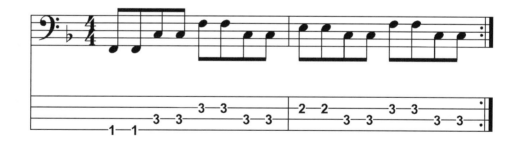

90.
Bb Major
Pop
Medium

91.
D Minor
Metal
Medium

92.
C Minor
Metal
Medium

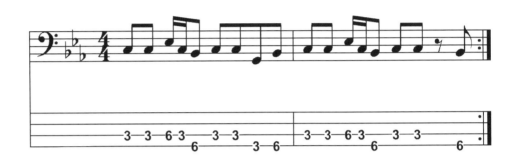

93.
C Minor
Rock
Medium

94.
C Minor
Funk
Medium / Slow

95.
A Major
Pop
Medium

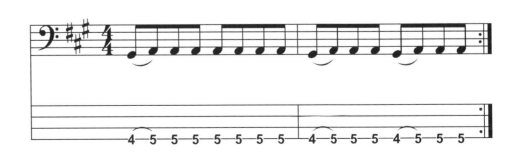

96.
A Minor
Rock
Medium

97.
A Minor
Funk
Medium

98.
C Minor
Pop
Medium / Slow

99.
A Major
Blues
Medium

100.
G Major
Blues
Medium / Slow

101.
G Minor
Blues
Medium

102.
A Major
Rock
Medium

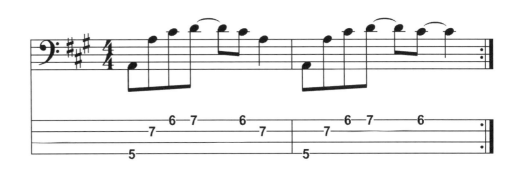

103.
D Minor
Metal
Medium / Fast

104.
C Minor
Pop
Medium / Slow

105.
G Minor
Funk
Medium

106.
G Major
Pop
Fast

107.
G Major
Pop
Medium

108.
G Major
Funk
Medium / Fast

109.
F Major
Pop
Medium / Slow

110.
F Minor
Funk
Medium

Section 3: Popular Tunes

This section of the book contains a selection of popular tunes arranged for bass guitar. Use them for sight-reading practice, to work on your technique, or simply to play for pleasure. Guitar chords are provided, so get together with a guitarist and play some music!

Amazing Grace

Traditional

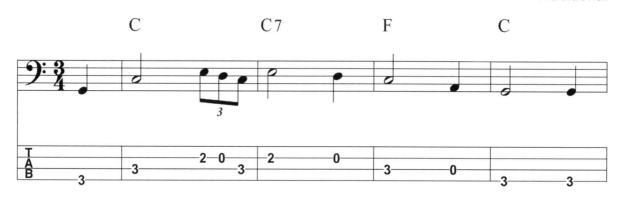

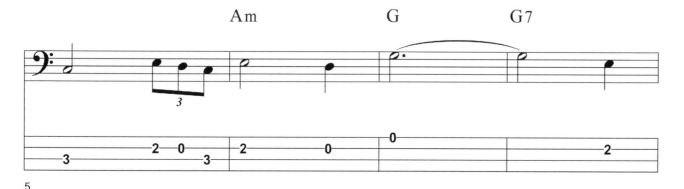

5

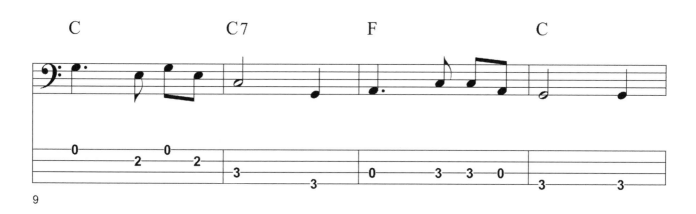

9

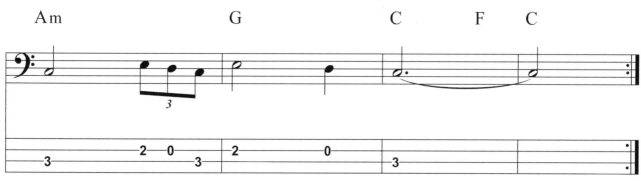

13

Ode To Joy

Ludwig van Beethoven

When The Saints Go Marching In

Traditional

Greensleeves

Traditional English

Home On The Range

Traditional American

63

We Wish You A Merry Christmas

Traditional English

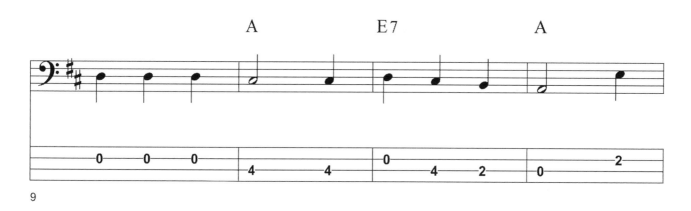

5

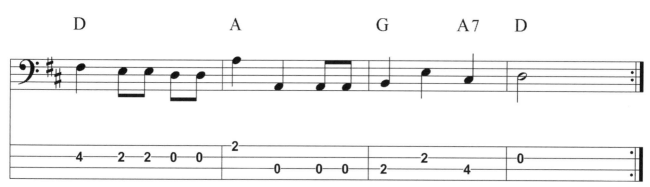

9

13

Scarborough Fair

Traditional English

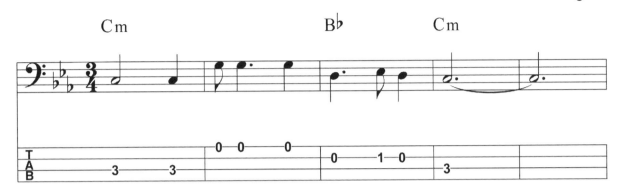

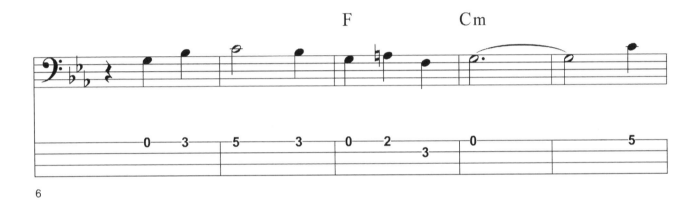

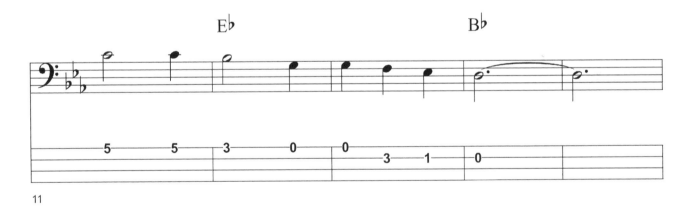

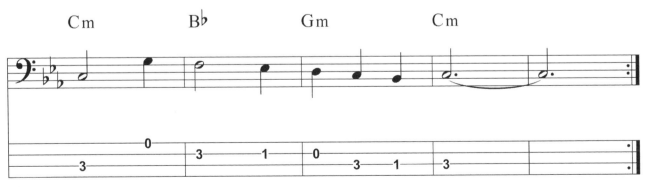

Auld Lang Syne

Traditional

Swing Low, Sweet Chariot

Spiritual

The Wind That Shakes The Barley

Traditional Irish

Londonderry Air (Danny Boy)

Traditional Irish

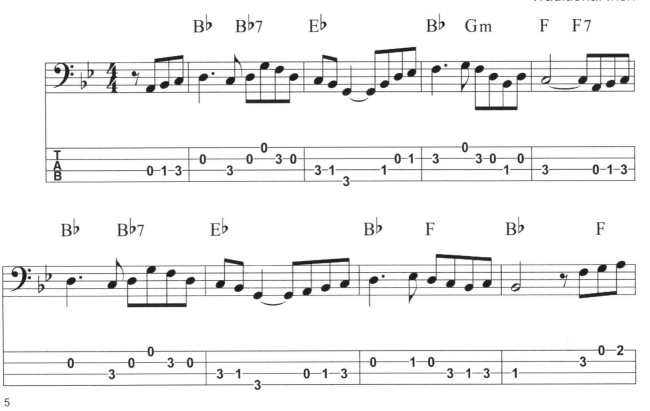

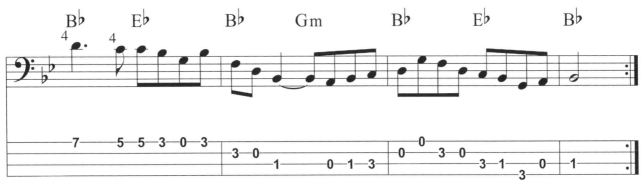

The Star-Spangled Banner

John Stafford Smith

Für Elise

Ludwig van Beethoven

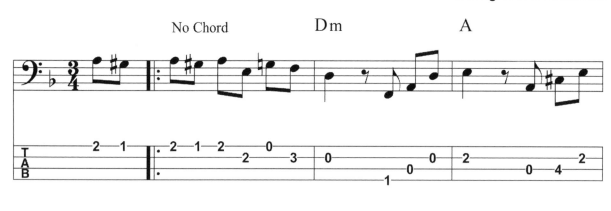

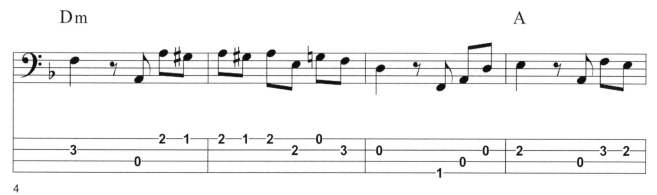

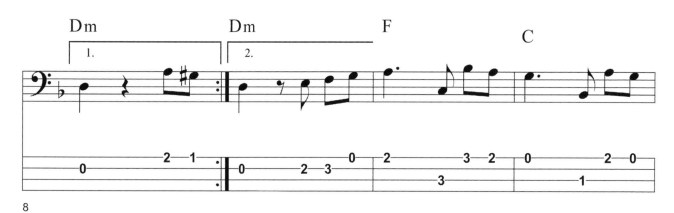

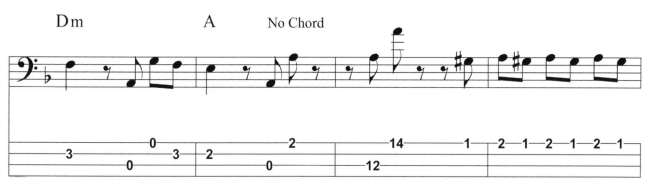

The Rakes Of Kildare

Traditional Irish

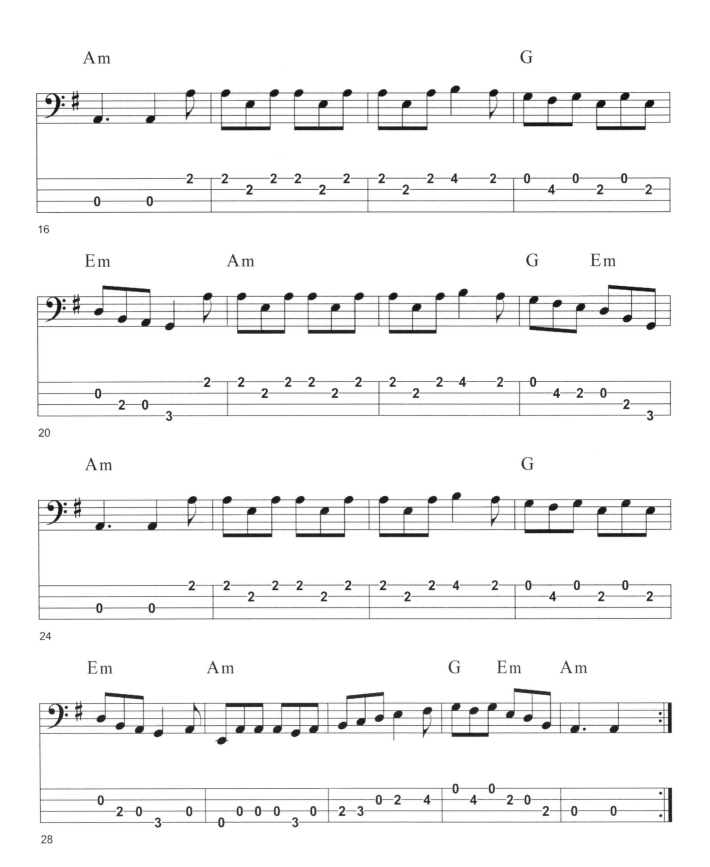

Largo (From The Four Seasons)

Antonio Vivaldi

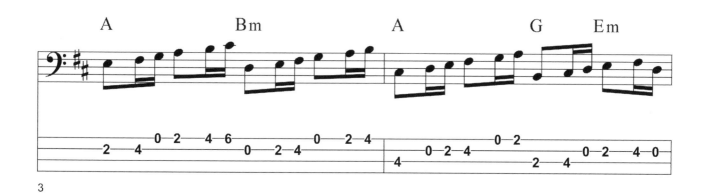

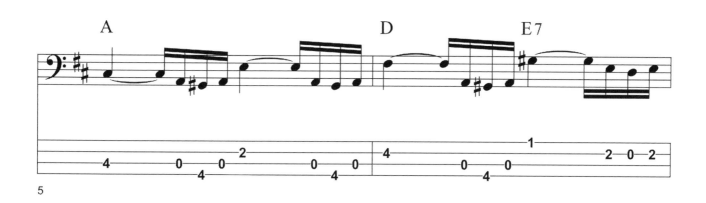

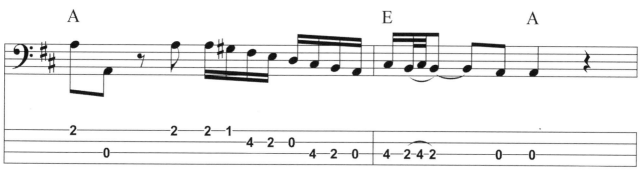

77

Other Guitar Command Bass Publications

Bass Guitar Backing Tracks

A range of high-quality bass backing tracks for practice & performance. Invent your own bass lines and improvise bass solos. The ideal practice tool for bass guitarists.

Backing tracks available for instant download from www.GuitarCommand.com, iTunes, Amazon & many other online stores.

Bass Scales, Chords & Arpeggios

An awesome reference book for all bass guitarists. Learn scales and modes in any key. Play bass guitar chords. Use arpeggios to create bass lines and improvise solos. The all-in-one bass guitar reference book.

www.GuitarCommand.com

Made in the USA
Columbia, SC
10 September 2023